Hey, Andrew! Teach Me Some Greek!

THE READER

A BIBLICAL GREEK PRIMER

BY KAREN MOHS

For my nephew

ANDREW VAN OS LATOUR

whose big round eyes
and precious smile
melt my heart

I love you, Andy!

ISBN-13: 978-1-931842-00-6
ISBN-10: 1-931842-00-0

Greek 'n' Stuff
P.O. Box 882
Moline, IL 61266-0882
www.greeknstuff.com

Revised 2/05

a

What's this?

It's an

ALPHA!

You could have fooled me!

It looks like an "a"
from my "A B C."

(Put your
finger here
and trace
the letter.)

(Alpha sounds like **a** in *father*.)

Double BUBBLE?
Bent BALLOON?
Big BUG with a tail?

No!

BETA's
a letter.
(But not for the mail.)

(Beta sounds like **b** in ***bat***.)

Going down, curving 'round,
way down there
below the ground.

Then up it swings,
a graceful fling.

GAMMA

makes me want to sing!

(Gamma sounds like **g** in ***God***.)

An EIGHT that is broken,
you say?

Almost right!

Our friend
the
DELTA
is a funny sight!

(Delta sounds like **d** in *dog*.)

δ

On to the
EPSILON!
We hop, skip, and jump.

Is it a FORK on its side?
Or a fallen TREE STUMP?

2nd   1st

(Epsilon sounds like **e** in *get*.)

ε

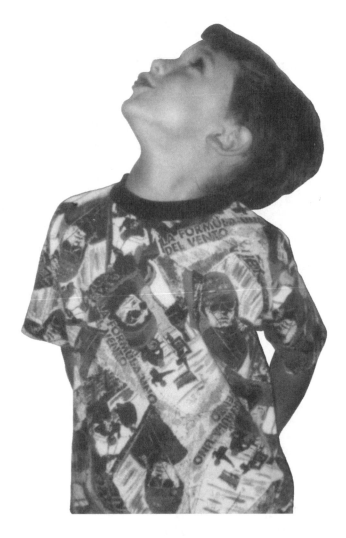

Can you see Captain's
HOOK,
way down below?

. . . At the bottom of
ZETA?

Go R-E-A-L slow!

(Zeta sounds like **dz** in *adze*.)

12

WHAT?

An "N" grew a tail
and escaped from the zoo?

THAT'S CRAZY!

It's an
ETA!

(Did it fool you, too?)

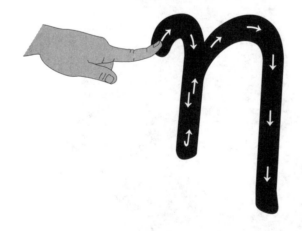

(Eta sounds like **a** in *late*.)

η

16

Cut a circle in half
from side to side.

A
THETA
you'll get.

Say it with pride!

(Theta sounds like **th** in ***bath***.)

A smudge on white paper?
Erase it right now!

HOLD ON!

It's slender
IOTA!

Please take a bow!

(Iota sounds like **i** in *pit*.)

Who shrunk the "K"?
Did you wash it on hot?

Of course not! You silly!

It's a
KAPPA
we've got!

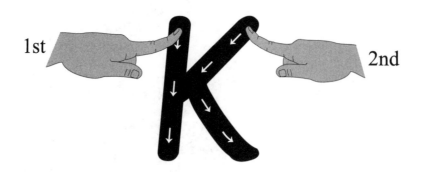

(Kappa sounds like **k** in *kite*.)

Κ

Is the "T" really falling
and hitting the ground?

NO!

LAMBDA's
the letter
and "l-l-l-l" is the sound.

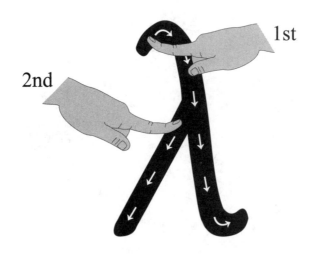

(Lambda sounds like **l** in *lamb*.)

λ

Was that a COW?
I just heard a
"MOO-O-O."

No, the cow's in the barn.
It's our Greek letter
MU!

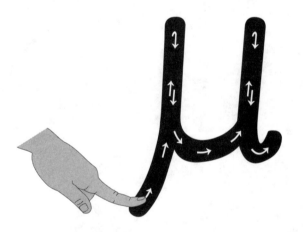

(Mu sounds like **m** in ***man***.)

What is NEW?
What is NEW?
Does a fly have the flu?

Nothing's new!
Nothing's new!

But our next letter . . .

NU!

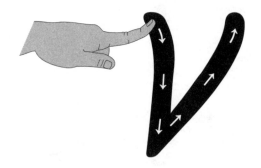

(Nu sounds like **n** in *nice*.)

Oh slithery, slimy, sickening!

Catch the WORM that's on the loose!

Worm? What worm?

It's a

XI!

You're such a silly goose!

(Xi sounds like **x** in ***box***.)

OH!
OH!
OH!
I'm SO, SO, SO
glad to see an
OMICRON,
a simple one to know!

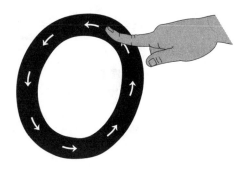

(Omicron sounds like **o** in *obey*.)

A table to put the goodies on.
Cakes and cookies?

WHY?

A PIE's the perfect treat to place
on our
Greek letter

PI!

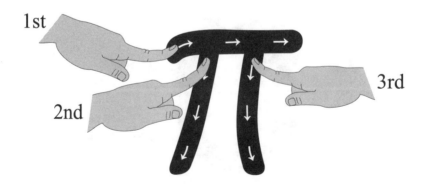

(Pi sounds like **p** in *pie*.)

ROW, ROW, ROW
your boat.

WAIT!

How can we go?

We have no water, boat, or oars . . .

Just our letter

RHO!

(Rho sounds like **r** in *row*.)

What's this we have?

Two letters here?

It may seem so, but NO-O-O.

They both say "s-s-s-s."
No difference - NONE!

SIGMA

takes the show.

(Sigma sounds like **s** in *sit*.)

A real T!

We're pleased to see
you stand so nice and straight.

A little short, but we won't fuss.

Mr.
TAU,
you look just great!

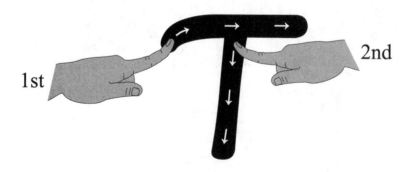

(Tau sounds like **t** in ***toy***.)

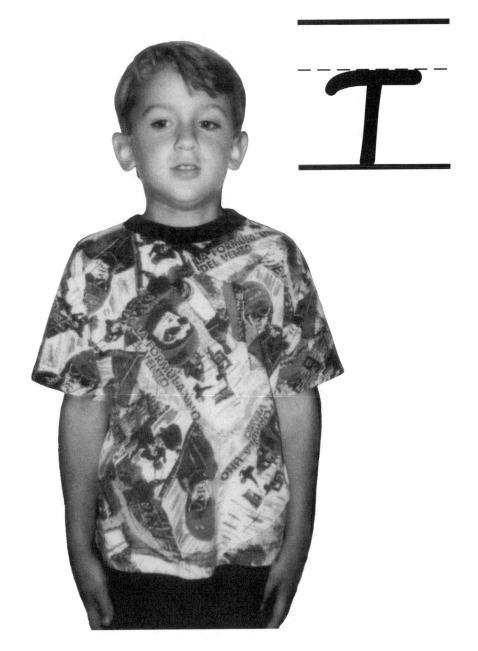

HOLD THE SHOW!
We've got to go
help this poor, sick letter.
You see, his sides are bending down.
Can someone make him better?

Better you say?
No way! No way!

UPSILON's

fine, with curving line.

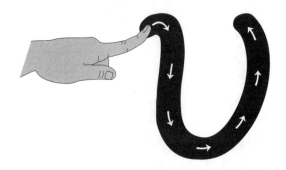

(Upsilon sounds like **oo** in ***good***.)

A BALL and BAT?
A CANE and HAT?

Not even close, I say!

If we need the sound
that our "f" makes,

PHI

will save the day.

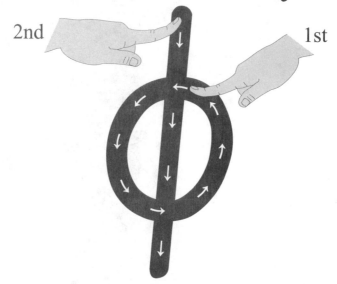

2nd   1st

(Phi sounds like **f** in *fun*.)

What's wrong with poor old X?

He slid right off the line.

I do fear he tripped and fell
and broke his crooked spine!

(No! X is not this letter's name!
And Mr.

CHI

is far from lame!)

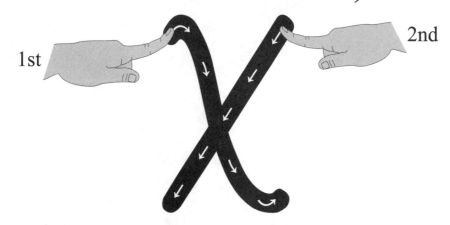

(Chi sounds like the German **ch** in *Ach*.)

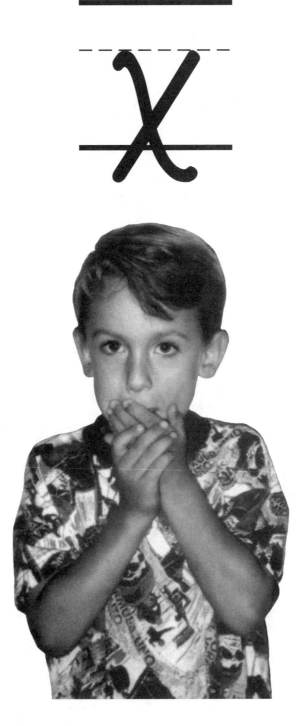

This letter makes me
squirm and pale.
Its point's so
LONG and SHARP!

Don't be afraid of gentle
PSI!
She's just a funny harp!

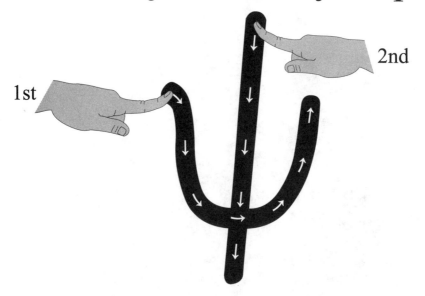

1st

2nd

(Psi sounds like **ps** in *lips*.)

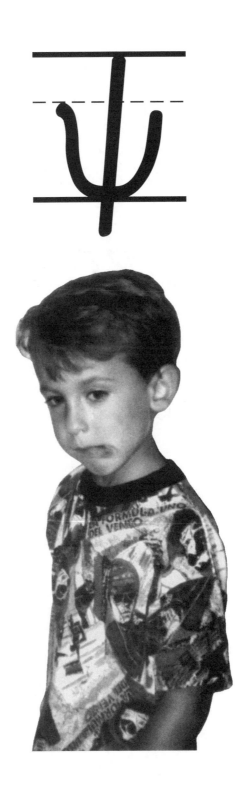

The last of all our letters,
like a "W" appears.

But
OMEGA's
had the "o" sound,
long and strong
throughout the years.

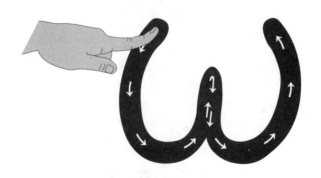

(Omega sounds like **o** in *note*.)

WHEW!

That was
FUN!

Now we can say

24

Greek letters
all the long day!

BUT

WAIT!

Why should we stop?

Let's put them together
and see what
we've got!

κύριος

54

The first we'll learn . . .
a most special word!

When we pray to our

κύριος,

we talk to our
LORD!

κύριος means *Lord*.

(κύριος sounds like **koo**-ree-os.)

ἐμοὶ

56

comes next.

It's not hard.
Please don't sigh!

Only four letters long,
the word's simply "my."

ἐμοὶ means *my*.

.

(ἐμοὶ sounds like e-**moy**.)

Do you like to help
your mom and dad?

A

βonθós

at home
makes everyone glad!

βonθós means *helper*.

(βonθós sounds like bo-ay-**thos**.)

βοηθός

That's terrifically GREAT!

Your sentence is done!

It's hard to think of a truer one.

Praise God!

He has helped you.

You're learning to speak
the Bible's own language
KOINÉ GREEK!

κύριος ἐμοὶ βοηθός

means

"The Lord is my helper."

(Hebrews 13:6)

κύριος ἐμοὶ βοηθός.

Dear Parent/Teacher:

Repetition, the key to successful learning, will be an enjoyable experience as well as a happy memory for your child as you read this primer together.

The pronunciation key found at the bottom of each page is listed below for your convenience.

Greek Alphabet

Letter	Name	Pronunciation
α	alpha (**al**-fa)	**a** in *father*
β	beta (**bay**-ta)	**b** in *bat*
γ	gamma (**gam**-ma)	**g** in *God*
δ	delta (**del**-ta)	**d** in *dog*
ε	epsilon (**ep**-si-lon)	**e** in *get*
ζ	zeta (**zay**-ta)	**dz** in *adze*
η	eta (**ay**-ta)	**a** in *late*
θ	theta (**thay**-ta)	**th** in *bath*
ι	iota (ee-**o**-ta)	**i** in *pit*
κ	kappa (**kap**-pa)	**k** in *kite*
λ	lambda (**lamb**-da)	**l** in *lamb*
μ	mu (moo)	**m** in *man*
ν	nu (noo)	**n** in *nice*
ξ	xi (ksee)	**x** in *box*
ο	omicron (**ahm**-i-cron)	**o** in *obey**
π	pi (pie)	**p** in *pie*
ρ	rho (row)	**r** in *row*
σ ς	sigma (**sig**-ma)	**s** in *sit*
τ	tau (tou)	**t** in *toy*
υ	upsilon (**up**-si-lon)	**oo** in *good*
φ	phi (fee)	**f** in *fun*
χ	chi (kee)	**ch** in *Ach*
ψ	psi (psee)	**ps** in *lips*
ω	omega (o-**may**-ga)	**o** in *note**

*The ο and the ω both have a long o sound, but the ω is held longer.